PRODUCING
AND
MIXING
HIP-HOP/R&B

mike hamilton

EDITED BY JONATHAN FEIST

Berklee Press

Vice President: David Kusek
Dean of Continuing Education: Debbie Cavalier
Chief Operating Officer: Robert F. Green
Managing Editor: Jonathan Feist
Editorial Assistants: Emily Goldstein, Rajasri Mallikarjuna, Claudia Obser
Cover Designer: Kathy Kikkert

"Beautiful Girls" Written by Boyce Uboh and Mike Hamilton.
    Produced by Mike Hamilton.
"Follow Me" Written and produced by Mike Hamilton.
    Vocals by Nadine Ford; Rap by John John.

ISBN 978-0-87639-085-6

1140 Boylston Street
Boston, MA 02215-3693 USA
(617) 747-2146

Visit Berklee Press Online at
www.berkleepress.com

DISTRIBUTED BY

HAL•LEONARD®
CORPORATION
7777 W. BLUEMOUND RD. P.O. BOX 13819
MILWAUKEE, WISCONSIN 53213

Visit Hal Leonard Online at
www.halleonard.com

CONTENTS

DVD TRACKS

Drums Tracks (1_Drums)
    Drums (1_Drums_MIP.wav)
    Boom Kick (Boom_Kick.wav)
    Claps (Claps.wav)
    Cymbal Crash (Cymbal Crash.wav)
    Hi-Hat (Hi-Hat.wav)
    Kick (Kick.wav)
    Loop (Loop.wav)
    Scratches (Scratches.wav)
    Shaker (Shaker.wav)
    Windchimes (Windchimes sample.wav)

Bass (3_Bass)
    Bass (2_DrumsBass_MIP.wav)
    Drum Bass (Bass.wav)

Guitar (4_Guitar)
    Guitar (4_Guitar_MIP.wav)
    Acoustic Guitar (Acoustic Guitar.wav)
    Funk Guitar (Funk Guitar.wav)

Samples (5_Samples)
    Enough Sample (Enough_Sample.wav)

Keyboard (6_Keyboard)
    Keyboard (6_Keyboard_MIP.wav)
    Keyboard (Keyboard.wav)

Background_Vocals (7_Background_Vocals)
    Vocals
    Hook Vocals 1 (Hook Vox 1.wav)
    Hook Vocals 2 (Hook Vox 2.wav)
    Hook Vocals 3 (Hook Vox 3.wav)
    Hook Vocals 4 (Hook Vox 4.wav)
    Hook Vocals 5 (Hook Vox 5.wav)
    Hook Vocals 6 (Hook Vox 6.wav)
    Hook Vocals 7 (Hook Vox 7.wav)
    Verse Backing 1 (Verse Bkg 1.wav)
    Verse Backing 2(Verse Bkg 2.wav)
    Verse Backing 3 (Verse Bkg 3.wav)
    Verse Backing 4 (Verse Bkg 4.wav)
    Verse Backing 5 (Verse Bkg 5.wav)
    Verse Backing 6 (Verse Bkg 6.wav)
    Verse Backing 7(Verse Bkg 7.wav)
    Verse Backing 8 (Verse Bkg 8.wav)
    Verse Lead (Verse Lead.wav)

Rap Vocals (8_Rap_Vocals)
    Rap Vocal Mix in Progress
      (8_Rap_Vocal_MIP.wav)
    Rap Ad Lib (Rap Ad Lib.wav)
    Rap Fill In (Rap Fill In 1.wav)
    Rap Fill In (Rap Fill In 2.wav)
    Rap Verse 1 (Rap Verse 1.wav)
    Rap Verse 2 (Rap Verse 2.wav)

Beautiful Girls Other Instruments
  (Beautiful Girls Other Instruments)
    Bouncy Synth (Bouncy Synth.wav)
    Splashy Synth and Lead Line
      (Splashy Synth & Lead line.wav)
    Square Wave Delay Synth
      (Square Wave Delay Synth.wav)
    Stereo Rhodes CP-80
      (Stereo Rhodes CP-80.wav)

Beautiful Girls Vocals
    Chorus Answer (Chorus Answer 1.wav)
    Chorus Answer (Chorus Answer 2.wav)
    Lead Vocals (Lead vox.wav)
    Main Chorus double/effects
      (Main Chorus double/effects.wav)
    Main Chorus/effects
      (Main Chorus/effects.wav)
    Rap 1 (Rap 1.wav)
    Rap 2 (Rap 2.wav)

Follow Me Other Instruments
  (Follow Me Other Instruments)
    2 Track no EQ (2 Track no EQ.wav)
    2 Track with Effect (2 Track with Effect.wav)
    Bass (Bass.wav)
    Bells (Bells.wav)
    Cymbal Crash (Cymbal Crash.wav)
    Guitar Octave (Guitar Octave.wav)
    Piano Pad (Piano Pad.wav)
    Ship Landing 1 (Ship Landing 1.wav)
    Strings (Strings.wav)
    Synth Chorus (Synth Chorus.wav)
    Verse Synth no effect
      (Verse Synth no effect.wav)
    Verse Synth w/ effect
      (Verse Synth w/ effect.wav)
    Whistle no effect (Whistle no effect.wav)
    Whistle with effect (Whistle with effect.wav)
    Wind Chimes (Wind Chimes.wav)

Final Mixes (Final_Mixes)
    Beautiful Girls (BeautifulGirls_FinalMix.wav)
    Follow Me (FollowMe_FinalMix.wav)

INTRODUCTION

A hip-hop/r&b producer has many jobs, but the ultimate one is to produce a finished product for commercial consumption. The producer's duties might include:

- Writing or co-writing

- Performing tracks, particularly drum tracks and keyboard tracks

- Working with other musicians and artists

- Using audio sequencing software, such as Pro Tools, Logic, Digital Performer, Reason, etc.

- Researching sound effects, samples, and other audio sources

- Editing and mixing tracks

- Mastering or coordinating with a good mastering engineer

In this book, we will explore all of these dimensions of production.

REFERENCE RECORDINGS

The best teacher for how to produce and mix hip-hop and r&b are the iconic records that have been recorded already. Getting used to hearing where a hi-hat is typically panned, how much reverb is on it, and how loud it is in the mix can give you more information than can be told to you. So one of the best things you can do, besides learning music theory and keyboards, is to have a record collection of contemporary and older hip-hop/r&b, so that you can listen to and dissect the music. I've included some of my favorite recordings in the appendix of this book. Also, top 40 lists of hip-hop and r&b are generated every year and can be found on the Internet.

TRACKING

Tracking refers to the way in which each instrument is recorded. The better the original sound, performance, and level, the less you will have to do to make it sound better in the final mix.

To track from MIDI, set your MIDI device's metronome to the desired tempo, and then in an audio recording program with the tracks set up to receive the MIDI input, click the Record and Play buttons to start recording. Many programs allow you to write in and edit MIDI parts. Either way, the important thing is to have the information recorded in your program.

There are different tools for playing back samples. Choose whatever tools you feel most comfortable using. In this book, I record my beat into Logic using Reason devices in Rewire mode, but you can use any system to try out these tools.

MIXING

Mixing is combining or blending volume levels, panning (location in the left/ right stereo field), and sound processing into one mass or mixture. Our goal in this book is to learn how to mix many instruments with vocals and sound processing to yield a typical hip-hop/r&b sound.

You can think of a mix as a series of transparent layers. You might have one layer right in front of you (loudest), another layer behind that (slightly less volume), and so on. You also have the top left and right, a bottom left and right, and a middle left and right. You can place different sounds in a mix in different layers, like pages in a book. We will explore how these layers typically look in a hip-hop mix.

Balance

A good volume balance lets you hear all the parts in the production. Nothing sticks out too much or is buried.

Panning

Panning locates the sounds from left to right in our speakers. We can go from 7 o'clock to 5 o'clock in the stereo field. This gives us a wide range to help separate the sounds throughout the field.

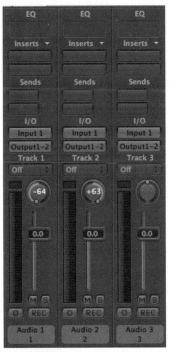

FIG. INTRO.1. Panning (Logic)

Sound Processing

Sound processing is used to alter a sound, clarify it, and sometimes both. When you process a sound, you try to match or blend it better into the song. Some sound processing is required to get the final product to meet industry standards.

Common sound processing tools include compression, equalization (EQ), reverb, and delay. They can be software plug-ins or physical devices, depending on your specific setup, but their use is similar. Use these tools as enhancers, but avoid overusing them, because they can give you the opposite of what you are after. It can be helpful to use hip-hop and r&b presets on your processing tools. These give you a place to start, and then small adjustments can be made.

Compression

Compressors are used to decrease the amplitude of louder signals and increase the amplitude of softer signals. By doing this, you may notice that you get more presence from the sound. This is because you are making the sound waves (which go up and down) come closer together, without the same amount of peaks and valleys. That makes the sound more consistent.

Compressor Settings for Hip-Hop

Most compressors have Threshold and Ratio controls. *Threshold* determines the level at which the compressor affects the signal. *Ratio* sets the amount by which the signal is lowered. For example, if a sound is 10 dB higher than the Threshold, and Ratio is set to 2:1, the compressor will turn down the volume of the signal by 5 dB. If the sound is at 20 dB above the Threshold, the compressor will turn it down 10 dB. Ratio settings range from 1:1 to infinity:1.

As you set the Threshold, you should look at the Gain Reduction meter on your compressor. (*Gain Reduction* refers to the difference in level between the signal input and output.) Adjust the Threshold knob until you get the Gain Reduction you need. A setting of 6 to 10 dB Gain Reduction is useful for drums, a shouting rap vocal, lead guitar, and background vocals. You will want to lower the Gain Reduction for other parts.

When you first begin working with compressors, it's often hard to hear the difference in ratio settings. A good place to start is to set the ratio at 4:1 or 3:1.

Creating Presence

Because most sounds naturally go up and down in volume, you occasionally hear them louder and then softer. Compressing a sound smooths out these jumps in volume so that there is a more consistent level of sound. For this reason, in hip-hop, a degree of compression works well on almost all instruments. It allows us to hear each sound as clear and stable.

Punchy and Tight

A compressor also makes the attack of a sound clearer. When we lower the louder part of a signal, the sound gets louder sooner and remains stable, so that we hear all of its elements intact. For this reason, kick drums and bass sound very good with compression on them. Again, try using a preset on your compressor, and then adjust each control so you can see and hear what everything does. If you don't have any compression presets, a good place to start is 3:1 Ratio and –6 dB Threshold.

Equalization

Equalization (or EQ) refers to the change in the level of certain frequencies of a sound. The generally accepted frequency range of human hearing is from 20 to 20,000 Hz. Changing any of these frequencies has a fundamental effect on the structure of the sound itself.

Let's take a look at two types of EQ: graphics and parametric.

Graphics EQ

With a graphics equalizer, you can turn all frequencies up or down by using volume sliders. Graphic equalizers range from five to thirty-one bands, each of which represents a range of frequencies. The more bands, the more control you have over each frequency. The graphic equalizer is easy to read since you can see the frequency range horizontally on the bottom of the front panel and the decibels vertically.

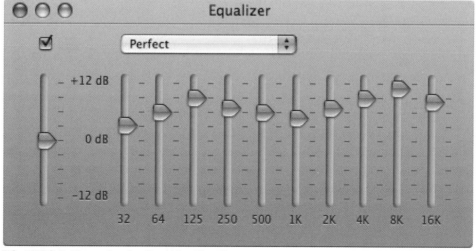

FIG. INTRO.2. Example of a Graphics Equalizer

Parametric EQ

To control a specific range of frequencies, you use *parametric EQ*. The range of frequencies affected by a parametric EQ is called the bandwidth or "Q." In Reason, there are two parametric controls on the MClass Equalizer. In them, you can sweep and manipulate frequencies from 39 Hz to 20,000 Hz with the FREQ knob. You also have control over turning the chosen bandwidth up or down with the GAIN knob.

In the MClass Equalizer, you will also find Lo and Hi Shelf parametric controls, which allow you to boost or cut a range of frequencies below or above a cutoff. The equalizer also includes a 30 Hz cut, which removes frequencies 30 Hz and lower.

FIG. INTRO.3. MClass Equalizer (Reason)

Let's take a look at a general frequency range chart.

Low Bass:	40 Hz and below
Bass:	40–200 Hz
Low Midrange:	200–800 Hz
Midrange:	800–5,000 Hz
Highs:	5,000–8,000 Hz
Extreme Highs:	8,000–20,000 Hz

- The low bass (40 Hz and below) is the subsonic low end and the very low range of 808 kick drums, regular kicks, and bass guitars.

- The bass (40–200 Hz) is the range that you control with the bass knob on your stereo.

- The low midrange (200–800 Hz) is the low mid-tone sound that is very unclear and muddy and makes for a very bad mix if not leveled out.

- The midrange (800–5,000 Hz) is very important because it's the frequency range that we speak in, and that most sounds around us are in. If you boost or cut too drastically in this range, you will make things sound unnatural.

- The highs (5,000–8,000 Hz) are the range that gives a nice top end to your mix. If you raise it correctly, you will achieve a clear and crisp top end to your mix. It is like the treble control on your stereo.

- The extreme highs (8000–20,000 Hz) contain the upper harmonics of sounds, such as cymbals and hi-hats. If you raise this range too much, you will make the sounds too abrasive.

Frequency Sweep

The best way to hear what a certain frequency does is to boost or cut it as much as possible. Using the GAIN knob, turn the frequency up or down to hear what it does to the sound. You can then move the FREQ left or right to hear which frequencies are changing. (This process is referred to as "sweeping the frequency range.") When you find the frequency you want, you can adjust the bandwidth, and boost or cut it to the correct degree with the GAIN knob. Then bypass the EQ in order to listen to what you had originally to make sure you like what you have done.

Reverb

Reverb is a type of digital signal processing algorithm that produces a continuous echoing sound, simulating an acoustic space such as a concert hall.

Delay

Along with reverb, *delay* is one of the most common effects used in production. You can produce a range of effects by delaying a source signal by varying amounts. The delayed signal is combined with the original, unprocessed signal.

AUTOMATION

Automation allows you to change instrument levels or turn effects on and off at different sections in your song. It essentially "writes" (real-time records or programs) the movements of a device's controls on a track during mix down. At playback, the controls (such as the Mixer's faders, panning knobs, and effects parameters) will move, as they follow the automation data.

AUX SENDS

Aux sends can help you save computer processing power. For example, we often find that we need reverb on multiple tracks. While you might add a new reverb unit to each track, doing so would load down your system and could cause it to crash. Instead, routing them all to a single reverb would be less CPU intensive. To set up aux sends, you need a "main aux track" that contains the effect that you want (e.g., reverb). Some programs refer to this track as a bus, as in Logic. In Digital Performer, it is called an aux track. Assign a reverb to this aux track, and name it something like "Master Reverb." This master reverb track has stereo inputs pairs that are identified by numbers starting from 1–2 and continue on.

Remember, 1–2 is a stereo image. Whatever you send to bus 1 will be a left signal, and what you send to bus 2 will be treated as a right signal. Then, any track that you send to "master reverb" or bus 1–2 from the track send will have reverb. You can increase or decrease the amount of reverb by the amount you turn up or down the send control from each track.

USING THIS BOOK

Going through these workshops will allow you to remix the recordings supplied on the data DVD using your gear. The sound processing parameters in this book were used to create these recordings in my studio; yours should be similar, but expect some variation. Use your equipment to get as close as you can to the sound you hear on the DVD. As you continue to listen for all of the elements involved with producing and mixing, your ear will develop a sense of effects, balance, and panning in a mix.

The workshops will discuss setup, listening, tracking, and effects processing as it relates to particular instruments. Once your mix sounds close to the reference mix provided, feel free to try some things of your own to see how it affects the overall sound.

This music was done in a home studio using a Korg Triton, Reason, Logic, Pro Tools, and a limited amount of plug-ins. Most contemporary digital audio systems will be capable of yielding similar results.

Hopefully, you can apply what you will learn here to your own projects.

Be patient. These things take a bit of time to get together.

Enjoy your music!

—Michael Hamilton

Creating a Hip-Hop/R&B Beat

The first song we will work with is called "Beautiful Girls." This song has a combination hip-hop/r&b feel. In this workshop, we will explore the drum tracks and go over specific settings. Then, you can experiment to create your own sounds with these tracks.

When producing hip-hop/r&b, I start with drums. Drums are the foundation of rhythmic music, and the drum part sets a deliberate intention as to how the music moves rhythmically. The drum beat strongly determines if the feel of the song will be heavy swing, straight funk, or an r&b feel.

When you have a great idea for a drum groove, you need to get the idea down before you lose it. I suggest that you start with MIDI sounds to create the essential groove patterns, and then "produce" (pick better sample sounds) after your idea is completely recorded. Otherwise, while you are looking for a great kick drum sound, you might lose the shaker part you were hearing, when you had the whole beat in your head. This is how producing and engineering have to be balanced to help the creative process.

You might find it helpful to store your drum sounds together in a special folder within your project folder. This will help you quickly finalize the exact sounds in your drum groove.

The screen shots throughout these lessons show settings using Reason and Logic. Since you are using the audio tracks on the DVD, your own sound processing tools will look different, but the settings will likely be similar.

WRITING DRUM PARTS

When trying to create a good drumbeat sound, keep these two things in mind: there should be balance between all components of the drum kit, and your listeners should physically feel the groove. It should make them want to tap their feet. That's what a hip-hop drum sound should be.

Learning to create hip-hop drumbeats begins with listening to the beats of great hip-hop music. Also, listen to the music that inspired early hip-hop: artists such as Parliament-Funkadelic, and many other soul/funk groups from the 1970s. See the appendix for my recommended listening list.

Hip-hop generally uses a funky backbeat. In 4/4 time, this means emphasizing beats 2 and 4. Some hip-hop grooves may also have a very slight underlying swing-sixteenth beat subdivision, although contemporary grooves are almost straight (very little swing).

What fundamentally sets hip-hop apart from other grooves is that the grooves are more syncopated than pop, rock, country, and so on. *Syncopation* refers to the emphasizing of a normally unstressed beat or beat subdivision. This characteristic is a big reason why early hip-hop artists often rapped over funk and r&b songs.

Getting a strong and confident kick drum and snare groove is the heart of the hip-hop beat. Here is my recommended approach to writing drum parts.

1. Set your hi-hat to hit on consecutive quarter notes, eighth notes, or sixteenth notes, with occasional 32nd notes (typically not played consecutively). Once you have a good solid beat, you can mix and match these durations. This gives originality and character to a drumbeat.

2. Set the snare to beats 2 and 4. Adding claps to this will strengthen your groove's backbeat.

3. Add a syncopated kick drum part.

Building a beat part by part, like this, is called "MIDI drum programming," as opposed to "sampling" (using a drumbeat or other sound from a different recording). Here's what the drum beat might look like in your sequencer.

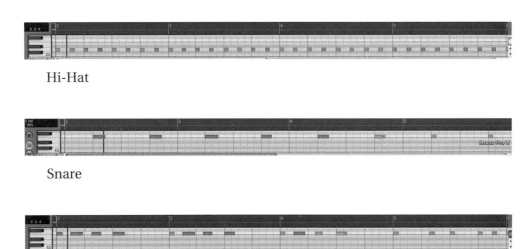

Hi-Hat

Snare

Kick Drum

FIG. 1.1. Drum Groove (Logic)

SETUP

In your audio program, add the following ten audio tracks. Your tracks may import as Stereo tracks. Once the track is imported select the type of track indicated.

Track Number	Track Name	Type
1	Kick	Mono
2	Boom Kick	Mono
3	Claps	Stereo
4	Hi-Hat	Mono
5	Shaker	Mono
6	Loop	Mono
7	Scratches	Mono
8	Cymbal Crash	Mono
9	Windchimes sample	Mono
10	1_Drums_MIP.wav (reference recording)	Stereo

FIG. 1.2. Beautiful Girls Drums (Logic)

Import the drum files from the data CD into these tracks. Also import the final mastered mix, "Final Mix," into the stereo audio tracks. All files are in the folder "Beautiful Girls."

LISTENING

Listen to the final stereo mix. (Mute the other tracks.) Focus on the drum sounds. Consider the following elements in how the drums were mixed to achieve the hip-hop/r&b sound:

1. The relative volumes of each drum and cymbal.

2. The cohesiveness of the beat, creating a very strong rhythmic groove.

3. The panning of each drum element in the stereo image, left to right. Which sounds are panned to which speaker?

4. The frequency ranges of the drums.

5. How EQ creates clarity in the drums, scratches, and percussion.

6. How compression levels the signal and gives presence to the instrument.

7. The reverb (ambient space), length (duration), and color (dark or bright), and how their application to the claps, shakers, and hi-hat gives ambiance to the mix.

Sound

Listen again to the final mix of "Beautiful Girls," and focus on the drums and percussion. Identify the rhythms of each part, and check out the balance, panning, EQ, and effects.

These drum tracks sound very strong and consistent, which is the foundation for drums in the hip-hop/r&b idiom.

There are two kick drums in "Beautiful Girls": a "boom kick" and a "main kick." The boom kick accents downbeats and gives the drone that is common in hip-hop. The main kick is the more traditional sounding kick that does most of the syncopated parts.

TUNING THE KICK

Hip-hop boom kick drums have a defined tone—not just a low punchy "thud," but an actual pitch. Tuning it is a critical part of getting the right sound.

FIG. 1.3. Tuning the 808 or (Boom) Kick Drum Channel 1 (Reason's Redrum)

To tune a boom kick drum, load the sound into your drum machine. Many MIDI sequencing programs have pitch or tune controls; check your program's section on pitch or tuning to see where your controls are. If your kick is already audio, you can check your audio sequencing program for an audio function that controls pitch, and tune it from there. Listen to the pitch that the drum produces once loaded. Check the "Do" (tonic note) of the song's key ("Beautiful Girls," in this case). You want to match these two pitches so that your boom kick is in the tonal center of the song's key. Most contemporary hardware, software samplers, and drum machines have a tuning dial on them. In Reason, the dial is called PITCH.

This avoids potential harmonic conflicts with the bass and other instruments with low frequency activity, therefore giving you tremendous clarity. You may not get the kick note exact, but the closer the better. If your bass line hits a note that clashes harmonically with the boom, don't use the boom at that moment.

SWING AND QUANTIZATION

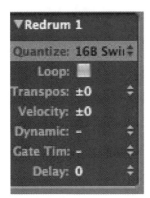

FIG. 1.4. Amount of Swing/Shuffle (Logic)

In contemporary hip-hop, the main kick drum and bass generally play slightly behind the beat. The way we get this feeling without actually playing behind the beat is to add a degree of swing (sometimes called "shuffle") to the kick drum and bass patterns. A greater swing value will make it sound farther behind the beat. In hip-hop, a 10% to 30% shuffle is common.

To lock in your kick and bass, use the same amount of shuffle on each.

In today's hip-hop, the hi-hat is usually straight. To shuffle your kick and bass only, put your hi-hat on a track that you can control separately.

This particular track has a swing setting of 20% and a quantization setting of 1/16.

BALANCE AND PANNING

Once your drum parts are programmed and their sounds are set, it is time for balancing and panning.

Begin by listening to the drum tracks one at a time (soloed). Focus on the relationships between each other to create the groove of the whole kit.

Alternate listening to the "Final Mix" track and to your current drum mix. This is called "A/B-ing" two sounds. In this case, you are using my "Final Mix" as a reference recording in much the same way that you might use a commercially released recording as a reference for your own track that has a similar sound.

Listen to the final mix, and compare its sound to the individual drum sounds.

Rebalance the levels by ear, and try to duplicate the volume and panning on the final stereo mix. Note that the individual mono drum files are still flat (without effects) so the sound won't be the same. Just try to match the final balance and panning.

Once you have achieved a good approximation to my mix, feel free to experiment and create your own mix. The next workshop, adding effects, will help greatly in matching the sounds.

CONCLUSION

We have discussed sound approaches to starting a project and keeping it organized as we build upon it. Discussing how to approach writing and producing will help you create and produce what you have come up with. Sound, tuning, and quantization are very important and will have a profound affect on the outcome of your project, so pay attention to these elements. Finally getting a balanced sound is what you will always look for—no matter how many instruments or vocals you add.

Drum Mixing

Once the groove is programmed, it's time to fine-tune the sounds using sound-processing tools.

KICK DRUMS

"Beautiful Girls" has two kick drums: the main kick and the boom kick.

EQing the Kick

Let's start with some typical EQing of our main kick drum to get it thumping. There are two EQ bumps.

FIG. 2.1. EQing the Kick (Reason's MClass Equalizer)

First is a 6.6 dB boost at 338 Hz. This adds some low mid-tone to the kick. These are typically taken out of r&b kicks but often boosted for hip-hop. The Q setting gives us control over the width of frequencies. Larger Q means more frequencies are included; smaller Q means fewer frequencies are included. Set this one to 13.0.

A little bit of attack was also added on this kick.

Second, there is a boost of 8 dB at 3,500 Hz. This is not always done for hip-hop; it is more common with r&b, to add punch. Set this Q to 9.4. You will find some hip-hop kicks with the 3,000 to 6,000 Hz area rolled off, rather than boosted.

If your kick does not have enough bottom, you can boost the 40 to 100 Hz areas with a small Q. This will provide big bottom, so be careful!

Always cut frequencies at 30 Hz and below to clean up the low-end rumble. In figure 2.1, you can see that the low cut indicator is on to cut below 30 Hz.

Note: Avoid raising the same frequencies on the kick that you will raise on the bass. This will help you obtain the separation needed for a good sound. Also, avoid raising too many different low-end frequencies on the kick, as this would lead to muddiness.

Compression on the Kick

FIG. 2.2. Compression on the Kick (Reason's MClass Compressor)

We will now add some compression to the kick to make it punch. I used Reason's MClass Stereo Compressor on the MIDI kick, but you can use any compressor with similar settings. Remember, different brands of compressors will have different results, even with the same settings.

Input Gain: 3.8 dB. This is the signal coming into the compressor.

Threshold: This is the level at which the compressor begins to act on the signal. As we turn the Threshold knob, we want to see no more than –6 dB Gain Reduction on the signal.

Ratio: 4:1. This dictates the amount of compression as well. This 4:1 ratio means the compressor will compress a signal that is 10 dB above the threshold by 2.5 dB. If the signal were 20 dB above the threshold, it would be compressed by 5 dB.

Attack: 39 ms. This tells when the compressor will start working on the signal. If you set this too fast, you will kill the attack of the sound.

Release: 84 ms. This tells when the compressor will stop working on the signal. If you set this too slow, you will keep the compressor working too long and make the next kick that comes sound over-compressed, or small and squashed.

You can make adjustments to these settings to get a slightly different sound.

MASTERING SUITE

FIG. 2.3. Mastering Suite (Reason)

We will also apply Reason's MClass Combinator Mastering Suite set on the "Hip-Hop" preset. This unit has presets that can be applied to a sound that you like as a touch up. Reputable software packages such as Reason, Logic, Pro Tools, Digital Performer, and Sonar have mastering suites with presets that can benefit your sound greatly. You may have to spend some time finding the right preset.

There are several plug-ins that come with mastering presets, and many of them add a nice touch to an already good sound. You have to compare what they do to get the ultimate sound you want. The best way to do that is to A/B the sound with a record you like—that is, to compare them, switching back and forth between playing one and playing the other.

REVERB

Some of today's records use a very small amount of reverb on the kick to give it more life. More typically, there is no reverb on the kick, but if you have no bass in your song, you may find it beneficial to use a small amount of reverb on your kick to make the sound seem bigger.

Center the Kick

The main kick is panned center.

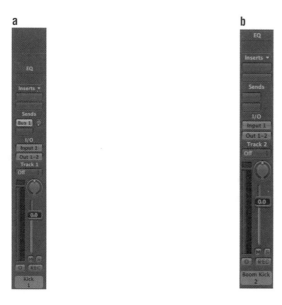

FIG. 2.4. The (a) Main Kick and (b) Boom Kick (both in Logic), and
(c) ReDrum Settings for the Boom Kick (Reason)

This boom has been "pitched" to C#—changed with the PITCH knob on track 1 in Reason's ReDrum machine to match the tonal center of the song. It was then converted to audio and put into Logic. It will not need any other EQ except cutting 35 Hz and below.

CLAPS

Look for claps that sound great to start off with. EQing the various frequencies may alter the natural sound of the claps. We are using the sample AIFF file "Raw claps" from Reason.

Panning Claps

Our claps are panned center so that the balance remains with the drums in the stereo field.

Claps Reverb

We will add reverb to the claps using the RV7000 "Small Hall" setting, because we don't want a huge, washy reverb. Contemporary drums have very little reverb on them, whereas large reverbs were used in the 1980s and would make our production sound dated.

FIG. 2.5. Reverb on Claps

Decay: 19
HF Damp: 18
HI EQ: 15
Dry/Wet: 36

The amount of reverb is determined by how much we turn up the aux send (see "Introduction" chapter) to the reverb unit. In this case, we will turn up the aux send halfway, giving us half of the entire effect we could use.

HI-HATS

The hi-hat in "Beautiful Girls" is a good WAV sample. It is pretty raw, the way we need it to be. There is not a lot to do with this hi-hat except make sure it is not too loud and that it stays raw.

Hi-Hat EQ

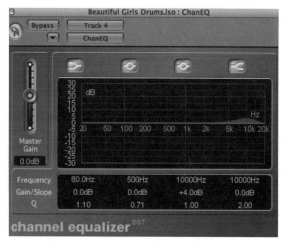

FIG. 2.6. EQing Hi-Hat on the Mixer (Logic)

We brighten up the hi-hat a little bit by using the channel EQ plug-in. We will give it a boost of 4 dB at 10,000 Hz with a Q of 1.00. This will add a nice sheen to the sound. Whether or not you need to do this will depend on the source sound. If you have a hi-hat that is really bright, you would not do this automatically.

Hi-Hat Reverb

We will use the same reverb unit as the claps and the same settings. This time, though, we will turn the aux up to about a third of the full range to the reverb unit. This gives us less effect on the hi-hat than what we applied to the claps, which were turned up to half. Add a small amount of reverb to your hi-hat, not a lot.

Hi-Hat Panning

The hi-hats are panned right at about 2 o'clock.

SHAKERS

Depending on your sound module, the shaker sound may be called a "cabasa." The important thing is to look for a sound that sounds authentic, not fake, before you render it to audio.

Shaker EQ

As on the hi-hat, we use the channel EQ in Logic. Raise the treble up to +2 dB at 9,600 Hz with a Q of 1.00 to get the brightness we need.

Shaker Panning

The shaker has been panned to the left at about 10 o'clock. This will give us some separation of our drums and percussion in the stereo image field.

LOOP

A small drum loop plays during the verse sections of "Beautiful Girls." It should be barely audible. This helps to thicken up our track, even though the part is not heard as a separate entity.

This sample has been edited from its original form, and it now contains a simple hi-hat and snare pattern that are not too busy. It has no EQ or effects other than the master effects on the whole mix.

Loop Panning

The loop is in stereo. It is the foundation of the track, so we need it to be big and full.

SCRATCHES

Scratches are a very important part of a hip-hop beat. They need to be a good sample or a good DJ scratching for you.

Scratches are placed into a beat to bring it to life, and give it a sound characteristic of the genre. Like the loop, the scratches are not individually effected.

Scratches Panning

The scratches are panned slightly right, at about 1:30. Use a mono track for this so that you can pan them.

CYMBALS

Cymbals give us the accents we need on sections of music that may be transitions or may need to be highlighted to give more excitement to the production. We always want our cymbals to sound bright but not biting.

Here are the settings for the cymbal crashes. Remember, all EQs don't respond the same. You may find that the Gain is more or less on different units.

Cymbal EQ

Boost of +4.5 dB at 8,100 Hz, Q of 1.80
Boost of +4.0 dB at 10,600 Hz, Q of 1.80

Cymbal Reverb

For cymbal reverb, I used Logic's Platinum Reverb Small Hall setting.

FIG. 2.7. Cymbal Reverb: Logic's Platinum Reverb

Use an aux send to access a "Master Reverb" (see the "Introduction" chapter). The percentage of wet vs. dry in the unit is as follows:

Dry signal: 91%
Wet signal: 10%

Cymbal Panning

The cymbal is panned to the right, but it makes the sound come almost center because the drum kit in Logic has this crash panned left already. So, I centered it more by panning it to about 3 o'clock. This also makes it sound further back in the mix.

WINDCHIMES

The windchimes sample has no individual effects. This sample blends very well as it is.

Windchimes Panning

The windchimes are panned center.

COMPRESSION

FIG. 2.8. Compression, with the Preset "Analog Tape Compression" (Logic)

Threshold: −12.5 dB

Gain Reduction: −5 dB

Ratio: 1.6:1

Soft knee: 1.0

Attack: 47.0 ms

Release: 170.0 ms

Gain: 1.5 dB

EQ

FIG. 2.9. Channel EQ (Logic)

Cut 30.5 Hz at –24.0 dB with 1.10 Q

Boost 9,000 Hz at +2.5 dB with 0.71 Q

Boost 12,800 Hz at +1.5 dB with 0.71 Q

CONCLUSION

The settings put forth will create a hip-hop/r&b sound and feel for your drums. You can make your own modifications to them, but keep them similar to mine for a good hip-hop/r&b sound.

High quality drum and percussion samples help a great deal because you don't have to use as much sound processing on them, but the discussion in this chapter will help you to enhance drum sounds that may not be of such a high quality. The use of panning, levels, balance, and effects have helped to keep this drumbeat in the genre we are striving for.

As we progress in our mix, we may readjust some of these settings to eliminate redundant frequencies between instruments. If we find our kick and bass bringing out the same frequencies, we will need to adjust one or the other to retain the best clarity for the mix.

In mixing hip-hop and r&b, the main objectives are clarity, balance, and making the mix "thump." We want to hear that the music is dimensional. Music should have depth, width, and height.

Bass

The bass's most important function is to play chord roots, supporting the harmony, and giving the groove a strong bottom end. Additionally, hip-hop bass lines are often clearly identifiable.

Bass and drums are the heart of the rhythm section and should work together as one.

SETUP

Import the bass track (bass.wav) to "Beautiful Girls" into your next open audio track, and label it "Bass." Try to match the volume level of the final mix.

FIG. 3.1. Mixing Board with Bass Track (Logic)

LISTENING

Listen to the "Final Mix," and pay close attention to the bass sound. Consider the following elements.

1. Compare the bass's volume to that of the kick drum. Is it louder, softer, or the same? Do the parts complement each other rhythmically?

2. Does the bass have any frequencies that stand out?

3. Does the bass volume change too dramatically in spots?

WRITING

Below is an excerpt of the written bass part for "Beautiful Girls." There are many good sampled bass sounds available. For hip-hop/r&b, try adding some of the vintage sounds to your bass sound library.

For this song, I selected "Pro Bass 3 Bass" from Logic's audio instrument, the ES1. Pro Bass 3 is a standard synth bass sound commonly used in hip-hop and r&b.

The bass line should always complement the drums—particularly, the kick drum pattern. That is not to say that they should always do the exact same thing. But, they should work with each other rhythmically to define the groove. This creates a strong sense of unity in the groove.

In hip-hop, the bass notes between chord roots usually come from minor scales. In addition to Aeolian (natural minor), the Dorian and Phrygian modes are common. Compared to the major scale (or Ionian mode), Aeolian has a lowered 3, 6, and 7; Dorian has a lowered 3 and 7; and Phrygian has a lowered 2, 3, 6, and 7.

The tonality of these modes is much darker than their major counterparts—something to remember when starting a song.

MIXING

Panning

Our bass will be panned to the center to obtain an even balance in both speakers.

Compression

Add compression to give the bass an even sound with a bit more presence. This will help create a dynamically consistent groove. It will also level the peaks and valleys in the bass volume.

Many effects plug-ins have presets to help you get started. Examine the presets in your effects and look for one that adds a bottom punch. Using Logic's Ultra Compressor A, I chose the bass compression preset "Bass Add Punch."

FIG. 3.2. Compression (Logic)

Threshold:	–6.5 dB
Ratio:	3.0:1
Gain Reduction:	–4 dB
Knee:	soft 1.0
Attack:	56.0 ms
Release:	250.0 ms
Gain:	0.0 dB

EQ

For presence, I gave the bass a boost of 5 dB at 2,600 Hz with a Q of 2.60.
To reinforce the bottom, I gave a boost of +4.5 dB at 91 Hz.

Bass Amp Plug-In

A bass amp plug-in simulates using a bass amp. It can give the warmth, drive, and depth of various bass amplifiers. On this track, I used Logic's Bass Amp Plug-in preset model Top Class DI Warm, with these parameters:

FIG. 3.3. Bass Amp Plug-In (Logic)

Pre Gain:	7.5
Bass:	5.0
Mid:	5.0
Mid:	2 (400 Hz)
Treble:	8.0
Output level:	−11.5 dB

Low Cut

Low cut helps us to keep our bottom end clean. Very low frequencies can tend to muddy up a production if they are not rolled off, and while we need a big bottom end for hip-hop, we do not want a boomy, muddy low end that will not deliver clear bass response.

Low cut devices cut all low frequencies below a set frequency range. Using Logic's Low Frequency Cut unit, 40 Hz and below have been removed.

FIG. 3.4. Low Cut (Logic)

CONCLUSION

We added our bass to the mix and tried to get an even level. The bass was panned to the middle to achieve the correct balance in the stereo field. We want our bass centered so the production will not sound lopsided or heavy to one side of the stereo field. Next, we added effects to enhance the sound and keep the mix clean and not muddy. In doing so, we used compression, EQ, and a bass amp plug-in. These techniques have helped the drums and the bass to lock together and enhance each other's performance, resulting in a funky groove.

Guitar

"Beautiful Girls" has two different guitars that are typical of the genre of hip-hop and r&b. Hip-hop guitar can include funk, rhythm, and picked styles of playing, and to a lesser extent, acoustic. Funk guitar was the first to be used in hip-hop music. Early rap songs were often made from existing funk, soul, and r&b records, so listening to artists like James Brown and Parliament will give you a feel for the style.

SETUP

Create two new tracks in your audio program:

Electric Guitar	Mono
Acoustic Guitar	Mono

Import the guitar audio files into these tracks, and try to match their volume levels to the final mix.

FIG. 4.1. Mixing Board with Guitar Tracks (Logic)

LISTENING

Listen to the "Final Mix," and pay close attention to the guitar sounds. Consider the following elements:

1. Where is the volume of the guitars in comparison to the bass and drums (louder/softer/the same)? How do the parts complement each other rhythmically?

2. The panning of the guitar tracks in the 180-degree spectrum.

3. The basic or core frequency response of the guitar. Do the guitars have frequencies that seem to get in the way of the other instruments?

Several companies have good-sampled funk, soul, and r&b guitar sounds to choose from. Some of my favorites are Glooped Downloadable Guitar Loops, Platinum Loops, Reason Refill Guitar Loops and Samples, and Loop Galaxy. I would recommend adding these sounds to your guitar sound library. Search the Internet for other guitar samples, and listen to them before you buy them.

I am using Logic's audio instrument, the EXSP24. For electric, I chose the Clean Electric Guitar 2 sound. This is a typical funk guitar sound that is used in hip-hop and r&b.

For the acoustic, I use the Steel String Acoustic 1.

The electric guitar accompanies the bass in unison in many sections to strengthen the line. It plays rhythm parts in the chorus to provide more rhythmic drive.

The acoustic guitar plays a small melody line to help outline the chords and to bring another color to the canvas.

MIXING ELECTRIC GUITAR

Sound Processing

EQ

We will apply EQ to give the sound some brilliance in the mix. Here are the settings for the EQ:

A boost of +8 dB at 5,400 Hz with a Q of 0.71
A boost of +3 dB at 8,100 Hz with a Q of 0.71

No other frequencies have been adjusted.

Compression

Compression will even out the guitar's dynamics, which will help create a more consistent groove. Compression also gives presence to the sound.

FIG. 4.2. Compression: Guitar Attack (Logic)

Threshold:	−15.5 dB
Gain Reduction:	−8 dB
Ratio:	4.6:1
Knee:	medium 0.4
Attack:	65.0 ms
Release:	160.0 ms
Gain:	−7.5 dB

Panning

The electric guitar is panned to 11 o'clock.

Effects

Overdrive

Overdrive is a common electric guitar effect in hip-hop. Its Drive parameter adds distortion. Tone lets you emphasize a specific frequency. Output is the level (volume) of the effect.

I am using Logic's Overdrive Hot Drive unit.

FIG. 4.3. Overdrive (Logic)

Drive: 17.50 dB
Tone: 3,300 Hz
Output: –10 dB

Chorus

Chorus is used to thicken guitar sounds. It is the most common of the modulation effects—those that alter a signal's wave. The chorus produces another almost identical note to the note being played. It then bends down one of the notes slightly and then returns it to the original pitch. The result is a modulation sound.

There are three common parameters. Intensity controls the effect's strength. Speed controls the rate of the modulation. Mix controls the amount of effect on the signal.

FIG. 4.4. Chorus (Logic)

Intensity: 10.0%
Speed: 0.500 Hz
Mix: 75%

Phaser

Like chorus, a *phaser* splits the signal into two parts. It combines the original signal with a phase-shifted version. The result is a wavy, spacey modulation.

I am using Logic's 12 Stage phaser.

FIG. 4.5. Phaser (Logic)

LFO 1:   0.22 Hz
LFO 2:   0.66 Hz
LFO Mix: 90%–10%
Sweep Ceiling: 14,200 Hz
Sweep Floor: 550 Hz
Stereo Phase: +70
Order: 12n
Color: 59%

MIXING ACOUSTIC GUITAR

Sound Processing

EQ

Boost of +2 dB at 5,500 Hz with a Q of 0.93

Cut of −2 dB at 350 Hz with a Q of 0.72

Compression

For the acoustic guitar, I am using Logic's Compressor preset Acoustic Guitar type 1.

Threshold:	−18. dB
Gain Reduction:	−1 dB
Ratio:	6.4:1
Soft Knee:	0.8
Attack:	1.0 ms
Release:	98. ms
Gain:	−1.5 dB

Panning

The acoustic guitar is panned to 2 o'clock.

Effects on Acoustic Guitar

Stereo Delay

Stereo delay can make a mono track sound like it is in stereo by panning the signal between the two speakers with a delay. It is possible to adjust the timing and placement of a stereo delay in milliseconds, allowing you as much flexibility as you need to get the correct effect. Most stereo delays show milliseconds as "ms."

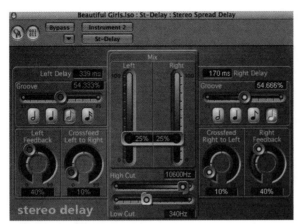

FIG. 4.6. Stereo Delay (Logic)

Left Delay:	339 ms
Left Feedback:	40%
Crossfeed Left to Right:	10%
Left Mix:	25%
Right Delay:	170 ms
Crossfeed Right to Left:	10%
Right Feedback:	40%
Right Mix:	25%

CONCLUSION

Each guitar has different functions. The electric is rhythmic and supportive. The acoustic is harmonic, melodic, and adds color to the overall sound of the mix.

The two guitar tracks are panned away from each other to give some separation of the similar sound. It also allows us to have a very wide and spacious sense of guitar in the overall mix and gives two guitar colors to each side of the stereo field. The guitars' clarity frequencies have been highlighted to separate them in the mix. The other natural frequencies have been left in to give body to the guitar and help the bass when the guitar doubles it.

Our mix will start to get denser from this point on, as we have added two instruments in roughly the same frequency area. When using effects, remember that sometimes the soloed track may sound overly effected, but this is typical. You will find that you may need to re-EQ tracks already in the mix as you add new tracks.

WORKSHOP 5

Remixes

Hip-hop/r&b producers often use a pre-existing song or loop to create a new song or version of an old song. We will use this approach in a new project, "Follow Me." This loop comes from a song called "Enough" and consists of drums, percussion, sound effects, and two different keyboard motif lines. The sampled track is our new song's basic music foundation. This is done often in hip-hop and r&b, as seen with songs such as "Juicy Fruit," which has been prominently sampled by The Notorious B.I.G. on his debut solo single "Juicy," Keyshia Cole on her hit single "Let It Go," "Loving You" by Jennifer Lopez, and "Faithfully" by Faith Evans. We will add vocals, strings, piano pads, and other elements to our loop to create a new song from it.

SETUP

FIG. 5.1. Mixing Board: Session Setup for "Follow Me" (Logic)

Create a new project, and name it "Follow Me." Add two stereo tracks. On track 1, import "Enough," which is the file Enough_Sample.wav. On track 2, import the "Follow Me" final mix file for reference.

Consider the following elements:

1. On drums, how can EQ help make the bottom frequencies sound correct? The top frequencies?

2. Where and how can compression help make the drums balanced and even?

3. On the keyboard lines, what frequencies must we cut or add to provide more clarity without hurting the sound of the drums?

4. Where and how can compression help make the keyboard lines stand out but remain even in the mix?

Note that we are limited in what we can do, here, because all of the sounds are already mixed together.

LISTENING

When you use previously mixed material, listen carefully to the original track. For our new work to sound successful, we may need to change the sound of the loop or sample track. For example, if we want to add bass and kick drum to the sample track, then we would have to remove some of the bass and kick drum that is already in the track by bringing down the lower frequencies. In our case, we want to use the sample track as the main foundation of the song, so we will need to make sure the track is strong and punchy. Some sampled loops that come on CDs or can be downloaded may not have the overall sound of a good mixed record, and you will need to beef up the mix.

1. Start by listening to a fully mixed song with similar instrumentation, and compare the two. You are listening to the overall sound of the mix and comparing it to your own sample or loop. My suggestion is to listen to the current top ten hip-hop and r&b songs on a contemporary chart such as iTunes' Top Ten List.

2. As you mix, listen to the amount of bass and the bottom-end punch—the overall brightness and level of the mix.

3. Use compression and EQ to get closer to the sound of the song "Enough" 2TRK with effects.

The desired final sound determines which effects you will use. In this case, we want to hear all of the sounds in the original song, so our effects will reflect that. But again, if we wanted to, for example, cut the bass part and kick drum and replace them with our own bass and kick, we would use effects differently.

SOUND PROCESSING

Compression

Compression evens out all of the instruments so that we can achieve balance. Then, we can enhance each frequency with EQ.

We are using compression lightly, here, just to even out the recording. By setting the Threshold at –14.5 dB, we obtain a gain reduction of no more than 5 dB so that the sounds will be reduced together, and therefore be able to be raised together more evenly. The 3 to 1 ratio is relatively mild, basically turning down the signal by one-third of the total dB once the level passes the threshold. Similarly, the attack of 26 ms is also soft so that it doesn't kill the instruments' attacks. The release is short so as not to over-compress the next sound.

With that in mind, here is one compressor setting.

FIG. 5.2. Compression (Logic)

Threshold: –14.5 dB
Ratio: 3.0:1
Attack: 6 ms
Release: 29 ms
Gain Reduction: 5 dB

EQ

We shape the original track by reducing annoying high and mid-tone frequencies and cutting muddy lower frequencies.

FIG. 5.3A. EQ: Low Cut (Logic)

This low cut device is set to cut all frequencies at 40 Hz and below.

For a big bottom, we boost our low end at 60 Hz by 1.5 dB with a Q of 1.80.

At 12,000 Hz, there is a slope reduction of –5.0 dB with a Q of 0.71 to smooth out the top end of the loop.

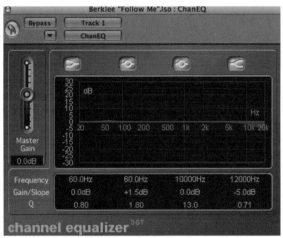

FIG. 5.3B. EQ on Sample (Logic)

CONCLUSION

The pre-existing song or loop is very important to the overall sound of the production. Much care must be given to keep it level. EQ'ing tracks such as these is a challenge, as you need to take into account many variables such as an enormous frequency range, with many different sounds that need to sound natural and clear.

When you subtract and add frequencies, avoid making the sound too thin or too heavy. Compression helps to even out the dynamic range a bit, and EQ allows us to bring down some of the extreme high and low frequencies that would hurt our production.

WORKSHOP 6

Piano

In this workshop, we will add piano to "Follow Me." Synthesizers and electric piano are commonly used in hip-hop/r&b. You will also find acoustic piano, vintage Rhodes, and Wurlitzer organ.

SETUP

Import the keyboard track for "Follow Me." This is a stereo track.

FIG. 6.1. Mixing Board with Keyboard (Piano Pad Track 3, Logic)

LISTENING

Adding this piano part will bring life to the whole track. The keyboard often serves as the harmonic filler in hip-hop songs.

Hip-hop chord progressions tend to be short, repetitive, and include seventh chords. Typically, they have between one and four chords, which repeat over and over. Because they loop, the transition between the last chord and the first chord needs to be smooth.

Listen to the final mix. Focus on the piano pad sound and think about the following:

1. The level of the part in the mix.

2. How the part fits into the song rhythmically.

3. The part's frequency range.

4. Any effects on the piano pad.

SOUND

Some commonly used keyboard patches in hip-hop include Rhodes, piano, and piano pads. Piano pads layer a piano with other sounds. These can vary tremendously, and can include strings, synth, bells, horns, and many other combinations of sounds. The piano is a base sound, however small.

Remember that you can use other sounds to play chords. However, because the piano is a common tool from which we compose songs, piano-like sounds provide a good place to start. Once you have this foundation, you can build on it by using other polyphonic sounds.

MIXING

Sound Processing

Compression

This setting will give a clear, strong piano pad sound that has some presence to it.

FIG. 6.2. Compression (Logic)

Threshold: –8.5 dB to achieve max 5 dB gain reduction

Ratio: 3.0:1 setting for one-third minus overall dB reduction

Attack: 19.5 ms for attack time to allow attack then compress

Release: 52 ms for release that allows signal to recover

Knee: Soft knee to gradually compress

EQ

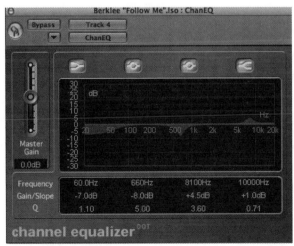

FIG. 6.3. EQ (Logic)

Low Cut:

40 Hz and below:	To clear the bottom mud.
Low shelf cut at 60 Hz:	To incrementally bring down some of the other lower frequencies that may muddy the sound.
Cut of –8 dB at 660 Hz:	To clear out the mid-tone mud.
Boost of 4.5 dB at 8,100 Hz:	To gain presence.
Boost of 1.0 dB at 10,000 Hz:	To gain clarity.

Panning

The piano is panned center.

Reverb

There is a "Small Hall" reverb on the sound, which comes from the keyboard itself. I really liked the reverb that was on this patch in the keyboard, so I decided to use this reverb from the source.

> ## TURN OFF EFFECTS DURING TRACKING
> It is best to turn off all effects when you are recording a professional project *unless you are sure of the reverb or effects that come on a particular sound*. There are many keyboards today that have excellent built-in effects on sounds, and you must use your discretion in choosing them or not.

CONCLUSION

The piano contains many frequency ranges and needs to be listened to carefully in order to make it fit into the mix. One of the most important duties of mixing the piano is to make sure you subtract the muddy frequencies without making the overall sound of the piano too thin. Compression will even the sound out by bringing all of the frequencies closer to the same volume. Then you have to take out what is making the sound unclear and boost a bit to help the presence and clarity of the sound. Add reverb to your taste.

Vocals

We now look at hip-hop/r&b vocals, from backgrounds to lead. We will see how to get them balanced and to stand out in a production. The vocals are usually the most important part of the track, so we will dedicate some time to going over them.

TYPES OF HIP-HOP/R&B VOCALS

Lead Singer

A great production technique is to record a good lead r&b singer improvising over the track. You can then take the vocals that you like and insert (cut/paste) them where your track needs some life. Some typical effects on a lead singing vocal are compression, reverb, delay, and EQ. The lead singing vocal should stand out against the rap and background chorus vocals, so use a different reverb and/or delay for each. You will generally have a larger reverb and/or delay on the lead.

Lead Rapper

Rap leads are often doubled to thicken up the sound. It is common for a rapper to rap the entire song two times and for the producer to use both tracks for the final record. Rap leads are clearly out in the front of the mix, and the vocals are compressed to help keep the level even. They are EQed to bring out clarity and the natural sound of the artist. Effects for the lead generally include a small reverb (not always the case in contemporary hip-hop, but more often than not) and/or delay and occasionally a bit of chorus.

Hype Track

A very common practice in hip-hop is to have a few tracks of the rapper ad libbing to spice up the track. There may be holes or parts in the track that are bland, and in those spots, a rapper may throw in a sound or words to keep the track interesting. These tracks can be manipulated in various ways with effects such as vocorder, distortion, and making the voice sound like it is coming from a telephone. This is where your imagination can run wild.

Background Vocals or "Shout Words"

It is common practice to find specific words that you want accented to strengthen either the message or the rhythm of the rap. When you have identified these words or rhythmic places, adding other voices will accent that part. Backgrounds in a rap song are usually compressed a bit and have a small reverb on them. You don't want the reverb to last long or be high in the mix. Pan the parts to give a wider sense to the sound.

Party Vocals

You will often hear what sounds like a party in a hip-hop song. To simulate this, you can get two or three people in front of a mic and record them talking and laughing. Do this on five or so different tracks, and you will have your party atmosphere.

SETUP

Add fifteen new mono tracks to the setup, and label them as shown. Then import the Chorus vocals without effects from the folder "7_Background_Vocals."

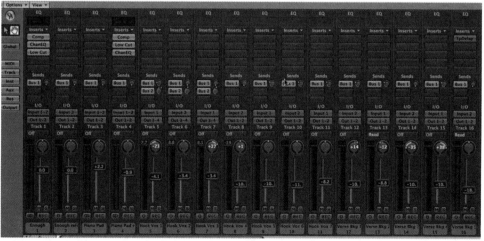

FIG. 7.1. Setup View for "Follow Me"

Track 1:   Enough.wav

Track 2:   Enough reference (mute this track)

Track 3:   Keyboard (Piano Pad)

Track 4:   Keyboard (Piano Pad reference) (mute this track)

Track 5:   Hook Vox 1.wav

Track 6:   Hook Vox 2.wav

Track 7:   Hook Vox 3.wav

Track 8:   Hook Vox 4. wav

Track 9:   Hook Vox 5.wav

Track 10:   Hook Vox 6.wav

Track 11:   Hook Vox 7.wav

Track 12:   Verse Bkg 1.wav

Track 13:   Verse Bkg 2.wav

Track 14:   Verse Bkg 3.wav

Track 15:   Verse Bkg 4.wav

Track 16:   Verse Bkg 5.wav

Track 17:   Verse Bkg 6.wav

Track 18:   Verse Bkg 7.wav

Track 19:   Verse Bkg 8.wav

Track 20:   Verse Lead.wav

Track 21:   Final Mix

LISTENING

Listen to the "Final Mix," and focus on the chorus or "hook" vocals. Consider the following:

1. The volume of the vocals in the mix (top to bottom and front to back).

2. The panning of the vocal tracks. Try and hear how far the parts are spread in the stereo field.

3. Listen for the blend of the vocals.

4. Listen for the clarity and think what frequencies could help to achieve that sound.

5. Notice the full round shape of the vocals in the mix.

6. Listen for any effects you may be able to distinguish, such as reverb, delay, chorus, and doubling.

VOCAL TRACKING

There is no substitute for a really good mic and pre-amp. A good mic will pick up a greater frequency range of the voice and send that true signal to the recording. Condenser mics have this characteristic. A microphone preamplifier's basic job is to take the signal from the microphone (low in voltage, with a weak current) and convert that signal into the voltage and current required for mixing consoles and recorders.

Some very good large diaphragm condenser mics for hip-hop and r&b vocal recording are the Neumann U87, Audio-Technica AT4060, AKG 414, and Shure KSM44-SL. (A microphone's movable plate, commonly referred to as the *diaphragm*, is the part of the microphone moved by sound pressure waves.)

Some very good pre-amps are the Avalon VT-737SP Class A Mic Processor, Focusrite ISA 428, and Behringer VX2000 Ultra-Voice Pro.

The proper distance to record a vocal is typically 10 to 20 centimeters away from the vocalist's lips. If you immediately encounter distortion due to the singer's volume, you should move the mic back before using any effects to help. You can also raise the mic above the artist, which has the side benefit of allowing them to read written lyrics more easily.

You will need to address sibilance, which is the overemphasis of certain consonants like s, sh, ch, j, etc. Here are some ways to do it in the order preferred.

• Use a de-esser unit—a special limiter responsive only to high frequencies.

• Simply try to get the artist to soften these sounds.

• Reduce the very high end with an equalizer, but be careful not to lose the rich high end that helps provide clarity.

• Use a high-pass filter.

Popping is another common problem when recording vocals. Popping is a significant jump in signal due to the pronunciation of letters such as b and p. To counter this, you can use a pop shield, though you may experience treble loss. An alternate technique is to place a stocking stretched over a wire coat-hanger a few inches in front of the microphone, which will also help prevent the artist from getting too close to the microphone. You can also put a piece of duct tape on the ground, marking where the artist should stand to get a good recording signal.

Record group background vocals in hip-hop/r&b in the same way you would most other styles of music. Simply get three to five people in front of the mic, and record two takes in mono.

Very often, we find a single singer or rapper doing all of the overdubs for a song. This is the technique we are using for this song.

You may need to make additional adjustments based on your own studio setup.

- All of the tracks from the "Vocals Follow Me without effects" folder will need to be started one measure and three sixteenth notes behind the other Files from "Show Me Audio." For example, if you start the 2TRK (Enough) exactly at measure 1, beat 1, sixteenth counter 1, then you will need to put the files from "Vocals Follow Me without effects" folder at measure 2, beat 1, sixteenth counter 4. The song tempo is 93.80.

FIG. 7.2. Event Float Window Showing Where to Start the Vocal Files for "Follow Me" (Logic)

- The vocals for this song were recorded on separate mono tracks with a Marshall MXL 2003 microphone, shock-mounted, with a pop screen. (A "shock mount" is a device with elastic shock-absorbing material that surrounds the mic on its stand.) There were no effects used during the tracking. All effects were added during mixing.

MIXING

We now need to route our effects for the backgrounds to an aux send so that we will not use up too much CPU power. (Reference your audio recording program manual on how to route aux sends.)

Create a bus for the following effects. We will then use the sends in the background vocal tracks to assign them to the background effects bus. From each background track, you can dial in the effects that are in the background vocal bus.

Here we will begin to listen to our reference track and start getting levels that are roughly in the neighborhood of our reference track.

With fewer instruments playing, you will be able to hear your vocals more clearly.

Panning

The panning used for these backgrounds were as follows:

Track 5: Hook Vox 1.wav. Panning: 10 o'clock

Track 6: Hook Vox 2.wav. Panning: 2 o'clock

Track 7: Hook Vox 3.wav. Panning: 9 o'clock

Track 8: Hook Vox 4.wav. Panning: 3 o'clock

Track 9: Hook Vox 5.wav. Panning: Center

Track 10: Hook Vox 6.wav. Panning: 9 o'clock

Track 11: Hook Vox 7.wav. Panning: 3 o'clock

Track 12: Verse Bkg 1.wav. Panning: 9:30

Track 13: Verse Bkg 2.wav. Panning: 2:30

Track 14: Verse Bkg 3.wav. Panning: Center

Track 15: Verse Bkg 4.wav. Panning: 8:30

Track 16: Verse Bkg 5.wav. Panning: 3:30

Track 17: Verse Bkg 6.wav. Panning: Center

Track 18: Verse Bkg 7.wav. Panning: Center

Track 19: Verse Bkg 8.wav. Panning: Center

Track 20: Verse Lead .wav. Panning: Center

*Other popular background vocal panning techniques include panning to the extreme edges of the stereo field and not having any background vocals panned center.

SOUND PROCESSING

Bussing Plug-Ins

In Logic, simply double-click on a bus (there are seven busses in the global mixer section), and it will appear in your .lso Mixing Board. We will add sound processing plug-ins in the inserts.

FIG. 7.3. Global Mixer (Logic)

We can now use the bus sends in each vocal track to add as much or as little of the bus 1 effects to the track as we want.

FIG. 7.4. Vocal Track (Logic)

Compression

Threshold:	−20.5 dB
Gain reduction:	4 dB
Attack:	9.5 ms
Release:	110.0 ms
Ratio:	4.0:1
Knee:	0.9

FIG. 7.5. Compression (Logic)

EQ

FIG. 7.6. EQ (Logic)

The following settings will clear muddiness in the lower and upper midtone areas as well as the bottom frequencies. The higher frequency boosts give clarity and sheen to the vocal.

Use a –24.0 dB cut at 60 Hz with a shelving curve using 1.10 Q.

–22.0 dB cut at 440 Hz with a 1.40 Q

+10.0 dB boost at 7,800 Hz with a 0.27 Q

+1.0 dB boost at 11,200 Hz with a 0.20 Q

EFFECTS

Reverb

Reverb gives our vocal tracks ambiance and presence. It also helps to settle the vocals into the mix better.

Pre-Delay: 20 ms
Reflectivity: 20%
Density/time: 100%
Room Size: 96
Mix: 30%

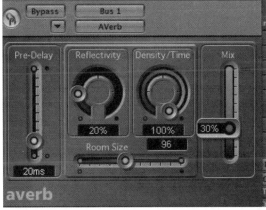

FIG. 7.7. Reverb (Logic)

Chorus

The chorus effect gives our vocal a sense of movement, even though you can barely hear it.

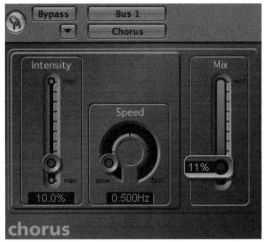

FIG. 7.8. Chorus (Logic)

Intensity: 10.0% not too strong to make the effect too much.

Speed: 0.500 Hz slow so it is not too obvious.

Mix: 11% again to barely hear it, but to hear it.

Sample Delay

Delay gives us more ambiance to the sound.

Delay L: 920 ms

Delay R: 920 ms

Link L&R: on

FIG 7.9. Sample Delay (Logic)

Readjust

After you have added these effects, you may need to go back and readjust levels. Your bus effects track should be at 0.0 dB.

The amount of send from each of your Chorus background tracks should be –15.9 dB.

*Remember these are settings used in Logic Express; you may find that your program requires slightly different settings.

CONCLUSION

The chorus vocals in the song "Follow Me" are contemporary, typical of what is used in today's hip-hop/r&b. Learning to mix vocals such as these will give you a very strong understanding of how vocals should blend in this genre of music.

SUBMIX NOTE

With this many vocal tracks in your session, you will need to bounce some of the vocal tracks down if you wish to add more vocals or instruments into the mix. There are different ways to do this, and it is best to check your audio recording program reference manual to see what will work best for you. In many of the popular audio recording programs, you can mix and pan the vocal parts as desired and then bounce them to a stereo track or a couple of stereo tracks within your session. How many tracks you bounce will depend on how much control you wish to keep with individual parts per track and how many tracks you have available.

Here is how to bounce (submix) in Pro Tools.

1. Create a new track in Pro Tools. Choose **FILE** > New Track from the Pro Tools main menu. You will use this as your submix track.

2. Set the input of your submix track to one of the buses in Pro Tools. Click the input on the track and select a bus from the list that you will see. You can use bus 1 for a mono submix or a pair of buses to make your submix track in stereo. Choose bus 1 & 2 for stereo.

3. Set the outputs of the tracks that you want in your submix. The outputs of the tracks that will be sent to your submix track must be the same bus or buses of the submix input that you set in step 2. Click the output for all of the tracks that will be part of your submix, and select bus 1 & 2 to make a stereo submix.

4. Record-enable the submix track.

5. Press the Record button on the transport to begin the mix-down process. Press "Stop" when you are finished and your submix is complete.

To bounce in Logic Express 7, you solo the tracks you want bounced and select Bounce from the master fader in the track mixer window. You can send the WAV or AIFF files to where you want, and then drag them back into an open stereo track in your session. You can add effects and bounce or bounce now and add effects later to the bounced stereo track.

Rap Vocals

Now we will work with the rap vocals on the song "Follow Me." In this workshop, we will see how to balance our rap vocals and get them to stand out in our production. We will examine the importance of effects and balance on these vocals.

SETUP

Import the rap vocals without effects from the file "8_Rap Vocals." After bouncing, your setup should be similar to this:

FIG. 8.1. Mixing Setup after Bouncing (Logic)

Track 1:   Enough_Sample.wav

Track 2:   Piano Pad

Track 3:   Bounced Hook Vox 5, 6, 7

Track 4:   Bounced Hook Vox 1, 2, 3, 4

Track 5:   Bounced Verse Bkg. 3, 4, 5

Track 6:   Verse Bkg. 2

Track 7:   Verse Bkg. 7

Track 8:   Verse Bkg. 8

Track 9:   Verse Lead

Track 10:   Rap Verse 1.wav

Track 11:   Rap Verse 2.wav

Track 12:   Rap Fill In 1.wav

Track 13:   Rap Fill In 2.wav

Track 14:   Rap Adlib.wav

Track 15:   Final Mix

LISTENING

Listen to the "Final Mix," and focus on the rap vocals. Consider the following:

1. The volume of the vocals in the mix (top to bottom and front to back).

2. The panning of the rap tracks.

3. Listen for the presence of the rap. How far away from the mic should the rapper be?

4. Listen for the clarity of the rap vocal. What frequencies could help to achieve that sound?

5. Notice the full round shape of the rap in the mix.

6. Which effects can you distinguish: reverb, delay, chorus, and/or doubling?

TRACKING

Mic Placement for Rap Vocal Recording

Rap vocals are generally more aggressive than other vocals. Because of this, you will need to make certain adjustments in mic placement and in the accessories used to achieve the best possible results.

The main problems we face for the lead rap include:

1. Shouting into the mic.

2. Tendency of the artist to move closer and farther away from the mic.

Remember issues addressed in workshop 7 about sibilance, popping, and mic placement.

MIXING

Balance and pan the levels similar to the final mix. Once you have the rap blended and panned, take a look at the effects that were used and start to apply them to achieve the proper mix.

Panning

Try spreading parts that are doubled left and right from each other. The ultimate idea is to spread the vocal throughout the stereo field without making any part stick out too much or sound too "alone." The stereo spectrum consists of the area from 7 o'clock to 5 o'clock. You want to spread the parts in different areas, much like trying to make sure you are using different low frequencies for your kick drum and your bass part.

Rap Verse 1.wav: Center
Rap Verse 2.wav: Center
Rap Fill in 1.wav: 11 o'clock
Rap Fill in 2.wav: 1 o'clock
Rap Adlib.wav: Center

Sound Processing

The following plug-ins are all on one bus to save CPU power, with the exception of delay.

Compression

Threshold: −25.5 dB

Gain reduction: 1–4 dB

Attack: 9.5 ms

Release: 98.0 ms

Ratio: 6.0:1

Knee: Medium Knee

FIG. 8.2. Compression (Logic)

EQ

−24 dB cut at 60 Hz with a 1.10 Q

−1.5 dB cut at 225 Hz with a 0.71 Q

Boost of 8 dB at 8,400 Hz with a 0.71 Q

Boost of 2.5 dB at 10,000 Hz

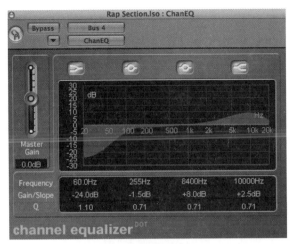

FIG. 8.3. Channel Equalizer (Logic)

Effects

Reverb

For this reverb, I used the "Ambience" preset. Check your program's presets to see if there is something similar to these settings, or program them in manually.

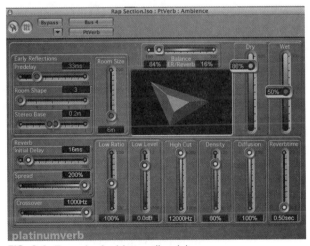

FIG. 8.4. Reverb: Ambience (Logic)

Automation: Delay

Some vocals have delay only in one place, such as the words "It's hot" at measure 88 and "Tear up the spot" at measure 90. Using automation, you can write in an effect and apply it only where you want to use it.

In most programs, you can keep an effect bypassed until you wish to use it, and then you can use automation to write in the effect for that section. You can also mute the aux send until you need the effect. Figure 8.5 shows Logic's TpDelay unit, indicating where the effect is active and where it is bypassed in tracks 13, 15, and 16. Check your audio program for more information about automating effects.

FIG. 8.5. Delay (Logic)

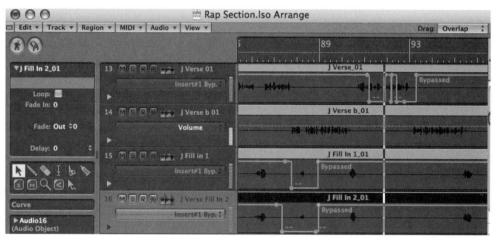

FIG. 8.6. Effects On and Effect Bypassed (Logic)

Once you have added these effects, you may need to go back and readjust levels. Your bus effects track should be at 0.0 dB.

The amount of send from each of your rap tracks may vary.

*Remember these are setting used in Logic Express; you may find that your program requires slightly different settings.

CONCLUSION

The rap vocals in "Follow Me" are characteristic of today's hip-hop/r&b. Learning to mix vocals such as these will give you a very strong understanding of how vocals should blend in this genre of music.

Mastering

Mastering is the final step in the production of an audio recording that renders the recording "ready" for commercial playback. This means that the audio recording will have very good response on a variety of playback systems. In mastering, you will improve your recording's volume level, balance of frequencies, noise reduction (if needed), definition, clarity, and depth. Hip-hop/r&b mastering is specific because the music has a stronger bottom end than most other music. When mastering this music you must remember that you need to maximize the low end while keeping the keys, guitar, scratches, etc. clear but not too loud. Vocals must be bright and clear out front while hi-hats are brilliant but not biting. These are just some of the things that must be considered when mastering hip-hop and r&b.

Mastering engineers often start out by going to audio engineering schools and then work for many years as mix engineers to gain the knowledge and experience to then master on a professional level. Also, a mastering studio's room and speakers are very important. You must have a good set of mixing monitors that are "true." *True* means the speakers, represent the true sound without enhanced treble or bass, and when you have that you can get a sound that once it sounds good on the true speakers will sound good on anything. The legendary Yamaha NS10s and newer versions are very popular for this reason. If you have a room that is not properly sound reinforced and has reflective walls you may get a sense of reverb that is not there, so that is one of the many reasons you need to have a room that is designed for mastering.

While an amateur in a home studio will not realistically be likely to achieve the same result as a professional, we can do some effective mastering in a home studio. Just be aware of the realities when you are deciding whether to pay to have your project mastered or to do it yourself.

Mastering is a science, and doing it well takes time.

SETUP

Once you have completely mixed "Beautiful Girls" and "Follow Me," create a new session in which to master the mixes. Use the following procedures to master your mixes, and then compare them with the mastered "Final Mix" files. (In your personal work, you can similarly use a commercially released recording as a mastering reference.)

Stereo Track 1	Beautiful Girls Mix
Stereo Track 2	Follow Me Mix
Stereo Track 3	Beautiful Girls Mastered
Stereo Track 4	Follow Me Mastered

FIG. 9.1. Setup (Logic)

1. Import the mastered versions of "Beautiful Girls" and "Follow Me." In stereo tracks 1 and 2, confirm that your levels for these tracks are at 0 db.

2. Notice the volume and the VU meter levels on the mastered mix as compared to your unmastered mixes.

MASTERING YOUR MIX

Master at a moderate level, not at a high volume.

The better your tracks are at the beginning of mastering the less manipulation in mastering will be needed.

Peak Normalization

Peak normalization changes the level of each sample by the same amount so that the loudest sample reaches a certain level, usually 0 to –0.5 dB. This gives you maximum signal over the full audio spectrum, but without distortion.

If you already have a very strong signal and can achieve a nice hot volume easily, then *you do not need to use normalization.*

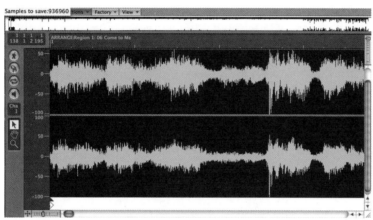

FIG. 9.2. Peak Normalization (Logic)

Mastering Plug-Ins

High quality mastering tools help fine-tune your signal without adding unwanted artifacts.

1. **Multiband EQ** allows you to raise and lower frequencies throughout the entire frequency range of your song. Start with a hip-hop/r&b preset, as a starting point. It should add more bottom end. Be careful, though, because if there is too much low end, you won't be able to raise the over-all volume where it needs to be to compete with commercial CDs.

These are third-party plug-ins.

FIG. 9.3. TL Audio EQ-1

FIG 9.4. Pultec Plug-Ins

Digital emulations of classic analogue equalizers, such as the TL Audio and Pultec plug-ins (above), often produce good musical results.

2. **Compressing** the whole mix is done to give the track a "tightness" and keep things from jumping out too much. Compression can bring more punch to the track. It raises the lower levels up closer to the louder parts.

Too much compression can make the mix lose its dynamics. Start with very light compression, and try a hip-hop/r&b compression preset.

FIG. 9.5. Waves C4

Waves' C4 multi-band dynamics plug-in will achieve good results.

FIG. 9.6. Universal Audio's 1176SE

You can also use a full-band compressor such as Universal Audio's 1176SE, if you're after a more vintage "pumping" sound.

The difference between multi-band and full-band compressors are:

    a. The full-band principle is where the entire audio signal is processed using gain control. When gain reduction occurs, the whole signal level is reduced. This is like turning the volume down on your stereo, so when you have a loud peak, it makes the compressor act no matter where the peak occurred, frequency-wise, and the whole signal gets reduced.

    b. With a multi-band compression, a loud event in one frequency band won't trigger gain reduction in the other bands, so if you have a loud kick drum, instead of reducing the whole mix, only the low-frequency sounds such as kick and bass will be compressed, and the compression will not affect the mid-range and high frequencies.

  3. **Limiting** can help to increase the volume of your mix by placing a hard limit on the signal. This can then be turned up to give more volume without distortion (unless really pushed).

FIG. 9.7. Limiter (Third Party Plug-In)

  4. A **maximizer** can also give a boost in volume while applying peak limiting, level maximizing, and dithering. Your audio program should have dithering when you are bouncing to disc. You need to dither if you are going from 24-bit high resolution to 16-bit in order to burn onto a CD. Dithering basically adds noise to the audio signal at low levels. This reduces distortion of low-level audio and extends the dynamic range at a given bit resolution.

FIG. 9.8. Waves L2 Ultramaximizer (Third Party Plug-In)

The Waves L2 Ultramaximizer can increase the overall level of your mastered track with surprisingly few audible artifacts.

Some mastering programs with good plug-ins and editing capabilities are Waves, Steinberg's Wave Lab, T Rex, and Universal Audio. Some include tools such as a spectrum analyzer, phase scope, and stereo imager. These devices help you to compare your own mix to a reference CD.

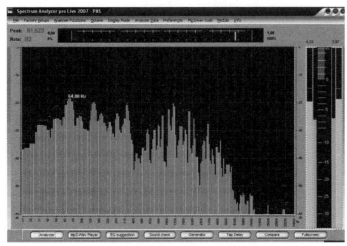

FIG. 9.9. Spectrum Analyzer (Third Party Plug-In)

FIG. 9.10. Phase Scope (Third Party Plug-In)

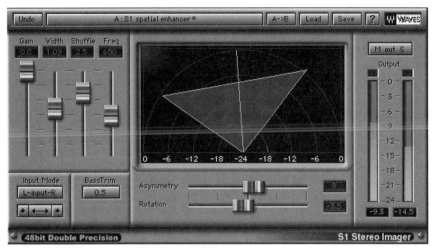

FIG. 9.11. Stereo Imager (Third Party Plug-In)

HOW TO MAKE YOUR CD SOUND COHESIVE

1. To make your album flow and keep the listener involved, put a couple of the best songs at the beginning of the CD.

2. Make sure that the overall EQ level is even throughout the CD—no bass louder on one song than another, no hi-hats sticking out on one song, etc. Listen to each song. If you hear differences in this area, address them in mastering.

    A spectrum analyzer will be very helpful in this. Try to match your mix to a reference CD.

3. Note any volume changes in songs. Use the VU meters to ensure that each mix is reaching the same volume levels. Again, match your tracks to a reference recording.

4. Take out any sounds at the beginning or end of a track so that you have clean breaks throughout.

CONCLUSION

Contemporary mastering plug-ins and programs are high quality and can yield very good results.

The order in which mastering processes are applied matters, and how they are used can make or break the mastering process.

Try to lay down strong solid tracks in the beginning, particularly vocals. Well-recorded, solid tracks require less work enduring mastering. Don't settle for distortion or things that can be "fixed in the mix," because usually, they can't. Organize your tracks so that they are easy to recall and work with.

Final Thoughts

When you have written/arranged/produced and are about to master, stop! Think for a moment, is it really good to do all of this by yourself?

While I have done entire projects on my own, I have found that they are better when I bring other people into the process. It is fun to see your vision come through, in the end, but getting it great because it touches many others is a different kind of magic. Working with others and including their input usually allows a larger audience to relate to and enjoy the music.

No matter how much equipment you buy and learn to use, a song is still about a good story, and about some sounds that are rich and vibrant and that flow well together. And yes, a bumpin' beat! So don't lose track of what brought you into it by trying to do too much.

Use your heart and ears to get your music to that special place, and have fun doing it!

—Mike Hamilton

Listening List

Parliament, *The Very Best of Parliament*, Universal, 2002

Funkadelic, *Young Soul Rebels*, Scotti Bros. Records, 1991

James Brown, *20 All Time Greatest Hits*, PolyGram, 1991

Chic, *The Very Best of Chic*, Rhino Records, 2000

Cameo, *Anthology*, Mercury Records, 2002

The Ohio Players, *Funk on Fire: The Mercury Anthology*, Mercury Records, 1995

Sister Sledge, *The Best of Sister Sledge*, Warner Bros. Records, 1992

The Isley Brothers, *The Essential Isley Brothers*, Legacy/Sony, 2004

Diana Ross, *Diana Ross*, Motown, 1976

Marvin Gaye, *Gold*, Universal Music Group, 2004

Earth, Wind & Fire, *The Essential Earth, Wind & Fire*, Sony/Columbia, 2002

Stevie Wonder, *The Definitive Collection*, UTV Records, 1973

Curtis Mayfield, *Superfly (Soundtrack from the Motion Picture)*, Custom Records, 1972

Isaac Hayes, *Shaft*, Stax, 1971

Isaac Hayes, *Black Moses*, Stax, 1971

Aerosmith, *Rockin' the Joint*, Columbia, 2005

About the Author

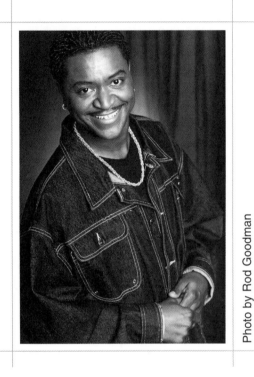

Photo by Rod Goodman

Mike Hamilton is a producer, multi-instrumentalist, and vocalist. He has produced and performed on recordings for Interscope and BGP Records, including *Heart & Soul* with the Winans, *Thus Spoke Z* with CTI, and his solo albums *Natural Attraction* and *Here Together.*

As a performer, Hamilton has appeared and toured with multi-platinum recording artists such as Ne-Yo, James Brown, Tyrese, Savage Garden, Coolio, Joe, Ronny Jordan, Jonathan Butler, and Phil Perry. He was a member of the house band for the Viacom network late night show *Live from L.A.*

He received his bachelor of music degree from Berklee College of Music where he became an assistant professor in the Contemporary Writing and Production department, and currently teaches at Berklee's online school, Berkleemusic.com.

Hamilton is founder of HMI (Hamilton Music Institute), a non-profit organization helping musicians of all ages learn to play, compose, and produce music.

For more information about Mike Hamilton, go to www.mikehamilton.net.

Berklee to Go.

Take your music career further. Learn about the future of the music industry. Discover how to set up a recording studio for that perfect sound. Strengthen your performance chops. You'll find all the tools you need with books and DVDs from Berklee Press.

DVDs ▼

A Modern Method for Guitar
Volume 1
Featuring Larry Baione and William Leavitt
14 hours of instruction!
A year's worth of guitar lessons at Berklee College of Music.

DVD-ROM $29.95   HL50448066

Basic Afro-Cuban Rhythms
Featuring
Ricardo Monzón
Learn the classic rhythms of Afro-Cuban music as master percussionist Monzón demonstrates the patterns and instruments that form its beating heart.

DVD $19.95   HL50448012

Harmonic Ear Training
Featuring
Roberta Radley
A vital introduction to ear training for songwriters and performers looking to improve their listening skills and become better musicians.

DVD $19.95   HL50448039

Jazz Guitar Techniques:
Modal Voicings
Featuring Rick Peckham
Extend your capabilities by integrating a variety of new voicings and articulations into your playing.

DVD $19.95   HL50448016

Jazz Expression:
A Toolbox for Improvisation
Featuring Larry Monroe
Learn to develop your own style as you work with the building blocks of expression and articulation to craft your personal musical interpretation of a song.

DVD $19.95   HL50448036

Jazz Improvisations:
Starting out with Motivic Development
Learn techniques for creating graceful solos from a two-, three- or four-note riff or motive. Add depth and variety by stringing several motives together.

DVD $29.95   HL50448014

Kenwood Dennard:
The Studio/ Touring Drummer
Find the right groove for any session or performance with one of the industry's most in-demand drummers.

DVD $19.95   HL50448034

Latin Jazz Grooves
Featuring
Victor Mendoza
Learn to apply your musical vocabulary and knowledge of rhythm, scales and chord progressions to explore this rich musical style.
Includes practice and play-along tracks.

DVD $19.95   HL50448003

Preparing for Your Concert
Featuring
JoAnne Brackeen
Learn routines and exercises to get you physically and mentally primed to walk out on stage and deliver an amazing performance.

DVD $19.95   HL50448018

Turntable Technique:
The Art of the DJ
Featuring
Stephen Webber
Learn about basic equipment set-up, beat matching, creative mixing skills, and scratching techniques like cutting, stabs, crabs and flares.

DVD $29.95   HL50448025
VIDEO $19.95   HL50448026

The Ultimate Practice Guide for Vocalists
Featuring
Donna McElroy
Learn to use the whole body to become the best singer you can be. Includes simple everyday exercises to increase vocal strength and endurance.

DVD $19.95   HL50448017

Vocal Technique:
Developing Your Voice for Performance
Featuring
Anne Peckham
Gain technical and expressive command of your voice while avoiding injuries and maximizing your vocal potential.

DVD $19.95   HL50448038

BOOKS ▼

Jazz Improvisation for Guitar
A Melodic Approach
By Garrison Fewell
Build solos from chord tones and melodic extensions, using guide tones to connect melodic ideas and "play the changes."

BOOK/CD $19.95   HL50449503

Vocal Workouts for the Contemporary Singer
By Anne Peckham
Warm up before you sing and continually develop the range, power, and expressive scope of your voice with this essential workout book and CD.

BOOK/CD $19.95   HL50448044

Berklee Music Theory: Book 2
By Paul Schmeling
The second in a two-volume series, based on over 40 years of music theory instruction at Berklee College of Music. This volume focuses on harmony and voice leading.

BOOK/CD $19.95   HL50448062

The Future of Music Manifesto for the Digital Music Revolution
By David Kusek and Gerd Leonhard
Discover the top 10 truths about the music business of the future and how you can benefit from the explosion in digital music, today and tomorrow.

BOOK/CD $19.95   HL50448055

Understanding Audio Getting the Most out of Your Project or Professional Recording Studio
By Daniel M. Thompson
Develop a thorough understanding of the underlying principles of sound. Learn how equipment setup affects the quality of your recordings.

BOOK $24.95   HL50449456

Recording and Producing in the Home Studio
A Complete Guide
By David Franz
This comprehensive guide will show you how to create the highest quality recordings by teaching fundamental production skills and engineering techniques.

BOOK $24.95   HL50449498

Voice Leading for Guitar Moving Through the Changes
By John Thomas
Berklee Associate Professor of Guitar John Thomas shows you how to voice lead both chord tones and tensions, and will help you add a new level of sophistication to your music.

BOOK/CD $24.95   HL50449498

Afro-Cuban Slap Bass Lines
By Oscar Stagnaro
Afro-Cuban rhythms are hot! This book/CD pack will teach you to play slap bass in seven popular Afro-Cuban styles.

BOOK/CD-ROM $19.95   HL50449512

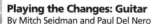

Playing the Changes: Bass
By Paul Del Nero

Playing the Changes: Guitar
By Mitch Seidman and Paul Del Nero

Each book/CD pack presents a unique improvisation strategy based on ear training and a linear interpretation of note/chord relationships.

HL50449510   HL50449509   EACH BOOK/CD $19.95

BERKLEE INSTANT SERIES
Absolute beginners can learn to play instantly with this revolutionary method! Each book/CD pack includes a wealth of playing tips, a jam-along CD and much more.

HL50449502   HL50449513   HL50449522   HL50449525   EACH BOOK/CD $14.95